Date: 12/21/18

ANIMALS AT WORK

Animals
Depending on
Other Animals

World Book, Inc.
180 North LaSalle Street
Suite 900
Chicago, Illinois 60601
USA

Produced for World Book, Inc. by Bailey Publishing Associates Ltd.

For information about other World Book publications, visit our website at **www.worldbook.com** or call **1-800-WORLDBK (967-5325)**.

Library of Congress Cataloging-in-Publication data has been applied for.

Title: Animals Depending on Other Animals
ISBN: 978-0-7166-2729-6

Animals at Work
ISBN: 978-0-7166-2724-1 (set, hc)

Also available as:
ISBN: 978-0-7166-2742-5 (e-book)

Printed in China by Shenzhen Wing King Tong
Paper Products Co, Ltd., Shenzhen, Guangdong
1st printing August 2018

Staff

Writer: Alex Woolf

Executive Committee

President
Jim O'Rourke

Vice President and Editor in Chief
Paul A. Kobasa

Vice President, Finance
Donald D. Keller

Vice President, Marketing
Jean Lin

Vice President, International
Maksim Rutenberg

Vice President, Technology
Jason Dole

Director, Human Resources
Bev Ecker

Editorial

Director, Print Publishing
Tom Evans

Managing Editor
Jeff De La Rosa

Editor
William D. Adams

Manager, Contracts & Compliance
(Rights & Permissions)
Loranne K. Shields

Manager, Indexing Services
David Pofelski

Librarian
S. Thomas Richardson

Digital

Director, Digital Product
Development
Erika Meller

Digital Product Manager
Jonathan Wills

Manufacturing/Production

Manufacturing Manager
Anne Fritzinger

Proofreader
Nathalie Strassheim

Graphics and Design

Senior Art Director
Tom Evans

Senior Designer
Don Di Sante

Media Editor
Rosalia Bledsoe

Special thanks to:

Roberta Bailey
Nicola Barber
Francis Paola Lea
Claire Munday
Alex Woolf

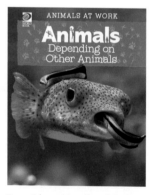

Two cleaner blennies pick dead skin, mucus, and parasites from this pufferfish.

Acknowledgments

Cover photo: © Hans Gert Broeder, Shutterstock

Alamy: title page & 12-13 (Bryan Knox), 5 (Wolfgang Pšlzer), 6-7 (WaterFrame), 7 (Reinhard Dirscherl), 9 main (Antje Schulte - Ant Life), 9 inset (Nigel Cattlin), 10 (Christian Ziegler/Danita Delimont, Agent), 12 (Pete Oxford/ Minden Pictures), 13 (jspix/imageBROKER), 15 (David Fleetham), 16-17 (James Forte/National Geographic Creative), 17 (Loren McIntyre/Stock Connection Blue), 18-19 (Jason Ondreicka), 19 (John Cancalosi), 20-21 (Norbert Probst/imageBROKER), 21 (David Chapman), 23 (Denis-Huot Michel/Hemis), 24 (Tim Zurowski/All Canada Photos), 24-25 (Bill Gozansky), 26-27 (Hans Lang/imageBROKER), 28-29 (Margus Vilbas), 30 (Steve Gettle/Minden Pictures), 30-31 (Anup Shah/Minden Pictures), 31 (Mark Moffett/Minden Pictures), 33 (Thomas Hinsche/imageBROKER), 34-35 (Photo Researchers/Science History Images), 35 (Michael Lynch), 36-37 (Paulo Oliveira), 37 (Juniors Bildarchiv GmbH), 40-41 (Piotr Naskrecki/ Minden Pictures), 41 (Mathieu B. Morin), 42-43 (Heather Angel/Natural Visions), 43 (Mike Veitch), 44-45 (FLPA), 45 (B. Mete Uz). **AntWeb**: 29 (Ryan Perry). **Shutterstock**: 10-11 (Kristel Segeren), 11 (Shane Gross), 22 (Brian Lasenby), 22-23 (Dr Morley Read), 27 (Karel Bartik), 38-39 (D. Kucharski K. Kucharska), 39 (D. Kucharski K. Kucharska).

Contents

Introduction

Every day, we depend on other people for our survival. We rely on farmers to grow the food we eat. We need manufacturers to make the clothing, tools, and other things we use every day. Workers rely on employers to give them money in exchange for their work.

Animals also depend on one another for survival. Some even rely on animals of a different **species** for food, shelter, protection, or other benefits. This type of relationship is called **symbiosis** (*sihm by OH sihs, sihm bee OH sis),* which means living together. Symbiosis takes many forms. Some times, one animal completely depends on another for its survival. Other times, the animal benefits from the relationship but can survive without it. In some cases, the two animals might be physically attached to each other. In others, they may lead entirely separate lives.

A common way of looking at symbiosis is to ask: who benefits from the relationship? When looked at this way, there are three main forms of symbiosis. In this book, we discuss each of these in turn. They are:

- **Mutualism (*MYOO chu uh lihz uhm):*** a relationship in which both animals benefit

- **Commensalism (*kuh MEHN suh lihz um):*** a relationship in which one animal benefits, and the other animal is unaffected

- **Parasitism (*PAR uh sy tihz um):*** a relationship in which one animal benefits, but the other animal is harmed

Examples of symbiosis can be found in all types of living things, including animals, plants, and **bacteria.** This book is only about symbiosis between different species of animals. We do not discuss human-animal relationships (see *Animals Living Alongside People* in this series), cooperation between animals of the same species (see *Animals Living In Groups),* or animals preying on other animals (see *Animals Attacking).*

The clownfish protects the anemone from predators by making a high-pitched sound.

The clownfish and the sea anemone

Clownfish have a mutualistic relationship with certain types of sea anemone *(uh NEHM uh nee)*. A sea anemone is an underwater animal that looks like a flower. Instead of petals, it has tentacles (feelers) tipped with stingers. The clownfish lives among the tentacles. It is protected from the stingers by a thick layer of **mucus** covering its body. The stingers help to keep away **predators** that would eat the clownfish. In return, the clownfish keeps the anemone healthy and clean by eating dead tentacles and **parasites.** Also, the clownfish's waste provides the anemone with **nutrients.** The clownfish can also scare away predators that would attack the anemone.

Mutualism: Food, Protection, and Shelter

Some **species** of animals have **evolved** ways of living with other animals for their mutual (shared) benefit. Often, each animal has a particular ability that the other animal does not have. These abilities work together to help both animals gain food, protection, or shelter.

HERMIT CRAB

The hermit crab is a type of crab known for making its home inside a discarded snail shell, which it carries with it. A young hermit crab will often attach a sea anemone to its shell, forming a lifelong **mutualistic** relationship. The anemone's stinging tentacles keep **predators,** such as octopuses, from attacking the crab. The anemone gets a number of benefits in return. For example, the crab will protect the anemone from its own predators, such as sea stars and fireworms, by attacking them or running away. An anemone moves very slowly and could not avoid such predators on its own. The anemone also eats scraps left over after the crab eats its **prey.** The crab also helps the anemone spread its offspring more widely.

Sometimes hermit crabs share their snail shell homes with tiny bristle worms. The worm eats **parasitic arthropods** called barnacles (*BAHR nuh kuhlz),* cleaning them from the crab's **abdomen.** In return, the worm has a safe place to shelter. It also gets to eat leftovers from the crab's meals.

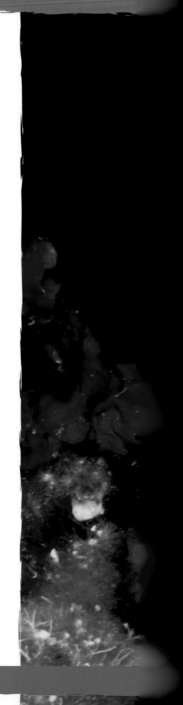

Goby fish and pistol shrimp

The pistol shrimp is an **arthropod** that defends itself by snapping its large claw shut. The snapping produces a powerful shock that can stun predatory fish. But the pistol shrimp has poor eyesight. For this reason, some pistol shrimps form a mutualistic relationship with a type of fish called a goby. The shrimp allows a goby to share its burrow. In return, the sharp-eyed goby acts as a lookout for predators. The shrimp keeps its **antennae** touching the goby. If the goby sees a predator approach, it flicks its tail several times, telling the shrimp of the danger.

This yellow prawn goby is waiting outside the burrow it shares with the pistol shrimp, watching for predators.

Hermit crabs will often carry more than one anemone on their back.

Ants and Aphids

Aphids (*AY fihdz, AF ihdz),* also known as plant lice, are tiny **insects** that feed on the juices of plants. Aphids make a sugary fluid called honeydew. Several **species** of ants rely on honeydew for food. The honeydew is so important that the ants have formed a **mutualistic** relationship with the aphids: they give the aphids food and protection in exchange for making honeydew.

The ants work like farmers, making sure their aphid herd is well fed and protected. When the aphids have drained a plant of its juice, the ants will carry the aphids to a new plant. If predatory insects or **parasites** try to attack the aphids, the ants will defend them. Some aphid species have become highly dependent on their ant "farmers." They have lost the ability to produce honeydew on their own and must be milked by the ants.

During the winter, the ants protect aphid **eggs** from the cold by storing them in their nests. In spring, the aphids hatch, and the ants carry them to a **host** plant to feed. In the case of corn root aphids, the aphids hatch before the corn, their favored host plant, has begun to grow. Their farmers, the cornfield ants, carry them instead to a smartweed plant, a weed that grows in cornfields in the spring. The smartweed acts as a temporary host until the corn starts to grow.

The relationship between ants and aphids may seem like an example of pure mutualism, as both animals benefit. But the ant is the more powerful partner, and it can use its power in ways that harm the aphid. For example, aphids can grow wings to fly to other plants. But ants may tear off aphids' wings to keep their "herds" from flying away.

The ANTS "milk" the aphids, coaxing them to release honeydew by stroking them with their antennae.

An ant defends its aphid flock from a ladybug.

SLOTHS AND MOTHS

The three-toed sloth spends almost its entire life in the rain forest treetops of Central and South America. About once a week, it makes the journey to the ground to defecate (*DEHF uh cate;* get rid of solid wastes, also called feces [*FEE seez*]). This can be a dangerous time, because coming down out of the trees brings the sloth in reach of **predators.**

So why does the three-toed sloth not defecate from the tree? It may be because of a **mutualistic** relationship the sloth has formed with moths that live in its fur. When the sloth defecates on the ground, the adult female moths leave the sloth's fur to lay their **eggs** in the feces. After the eggs hatch, the moth **larvae** eat the feces. So the moths benefit from the sloth's bathroom habits, but how do the moths help the sloth?

After the moth larvae become adults, they fly up into the trees to settle in the fur of a sloth.

The answer lies in the **algae** that grow on the sloth's fur. The sloths eat this algae to round out their diet of leaves and fruits. Algae are easy to digest and much richer in fats than are leaves. The green algae also helps the sloth to hide among the leaves from predators.

Some scientists think the moths help the algae grow by bringing them **nutrients** in their wastes and leftover food. Also, when the moths die, **fungi** in the sloth fur helps break down the moths' bodies, producing more nutrients for the algae. In this three-way mutualism, the moths benefit the algae, and the algae benefit the sloth.

Remoras

Remoras are a type of fish that attach themselves to sharks, whales, and other large ocean-dwelling animals. The attachment gives a remora transportation—it can move around the ocean without using much energy. The remora also gains protection from predators by its closeness to the larger animal. Also, it can eat the scraps left over by its **host**. In return, the remora cleans its host's surface of **parasites.**

Remoras attach themselves to their hosts using an oval-shaped sucker at the top of their heads.

The journey to the ground uses a lot of energy, around 8 percent of the sloth's daily calories.

Mutualism: Cleaning for Food

Many **species** enjoy a simple form of **mutualism.** These species offer cleaning services to larger animals in return for food. The cleaners eat **parasites** and other nutritious debris from the surface of the larger animal, known as the **client.** This form of mutualism is common among fish, but also exists among some birds and land animals.

CLEANER BIRDS

Some **insect**-eating birds live closely with large **mammals.** They eat the parasites that land on their clients, benefiting both bird and mammal. In the South American nation of Brazil, such birds include the black caracara, wattled jacana, shiny cowbird, and cattle tyrant. These birds land on the backs of giant **rodents** called capybaras (*kap uh BAHR uhz*) and pick off ticks, horseflies, and other parasites they find there.

A capybara with a cattle tyrant on its back.

BANDED MONGOOSE AND WARTHOG

In the east-central African countries of Kenya and Uganda, a small mammal known as the banded mongoose offers a cleaning service to warthogs. The warthog, typically a fierce animal, becomes unusually peaceful. It allows the mongooses to climb over its body, dining on the hundreds of ticks and other parasites that live on its skin.

PSEUDOSCORPION AND PACKRAT

The pseudoscorpion (*soo doh SKAWR pee uhn),* a type of **arachnid,** lives closely with certain kinds of packrat. Two pseudoscorpion species eat fleas living on the packrats—offering cleaning services in exchange for a meal of fleas.

Oxpecker: mutualism or parasitism?

The oxpecker is a bird that lives in **sub-Saharan Africa.** It perches on large animals—such as antelope, wildebeests, hippopotamuses, impalas, and zebras—and eats ticks and other parasites from their hides. The relationship between the oxpecker and its **host** was originally believed to be one of mutualism. But, some scientists now think that oxpeckers may be more like parasites. Oxpeckers sometimes make wounds bigger—and even open new ones—to drink their hosts' blood.

An oxpecker perched on an impala.

Banded mongooses cleaning parasites from a warthog.

Undersea Cleaning Stations

Some **species** of fish eat nutritious **parasites,** dead skin, **algae,** and other material from the skin of larger fish. These fish set up "cleaning stations" on coral reefs. **Client** fish arrive at the station and use special movements to signal that they wish to be cleaned.

Cleaner fish include species of wrasse, gobies, cichlids (*SIHK lihdz)*, catfish, tang, and surgeonfish. Cleaner fish of various species often have blue and yellow coloring, which may be a way of signaling to client fish that they offer a cleaning service.

Cleaner fish feed mostly on parasites living on their clients. But sometimes they will also nibble on the client fish's **mucus** coating and scales, as these have greater nutritional value. In this way, a **mutualistic** relationship can become partly **parasitic.** The cleaner must be careful, though. If it takes too much mucus and **tissue,** the client will end the cleaning session.

Some fish **mimic** the shape and coloration of cleaner fish to get a meal. For example, the bluestriped fangblenny looks enough like a cleaner wrasse to get close to a client fish. But instead of removing parasites, the fangblenny eats the client's flesh and scales. The presence of mimics near cleaning stations can harm the relationship between cleaner and client because it makes the client fish more cautious.

The CLEANER WRASSE, found among the coral reefs of the Indian and Pacific Oceans, eats parasites on the skin and inside the gills and mouth of its clients. The client fish, who might otherwise see the wrasse as prey, open their mouths to allow the wrasse to swim in and feed.

Commensalism for Transportation and Shelter

Animals that benefit from animals of another **species** without helping or harming those animals are known as **commensals** (*kuh MEHN suhlz*). The other animal (the **host**) in this kind of relationship may not even be aware of the commensal. In this section, you will read about commensals that get transportation and shelter (and often food as well) from another species.

WHALE BARNACLES

Barnacles are **arthropods** that attach themselves to a solid surface, staying in that spot for the rest of their lives. Barnacles may bind themselves to rocks or ships. But some species of barnacle attach themselves to whales. The whale provides transportation through the world's oceans, giving the barnacles far more feeding opportunities than they would have otherwise. Although adult barnacles are unable to move, they begin life as swimming **larvae.** The larvae use their front **antennae** to move themselves around the whale's body, seeking a good place to settle. Barnacles tend to favor the head or fins of the whale, where there is a steady flow of water to bring them the tiny living things they eat. Once a barnacle has found a good spot, it attaches itself firmly to the whale's skin.

A barnacle-covered gray whale. Usually, the barnacles on a whale do not affect it much. But if a whale becomes covered with too many barnacles, it could make it harder for the whale to move. It may also make it easier for the whale to get an infection. The normal activities of a healthy whale often knock barnacles from its skin, though.

Hitching a ride

A species of pseudoscorpion from Central and South America moves around the rain forest by catching rides on beetles. These pseudoscorpions live in the rotting wood of fallen fig trees. Once the wood has rotted away, the pseudoscorpions must find another tree on which to live. They do this with the help of the harlequin (*HAHR luh kihn*) beetle. This **insect** also likes the soft wood of rotting fig trees, especially as a place to lay its **eggs.**

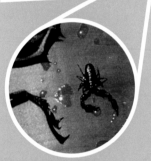

When the harlequin larvae grow into adults, they are ready to leave the tree. They are quickly surrounded by pseudoscorpions looking for a ride. The tiny **arachnids** use their claws to pinch at the beetle's belly. This causes the beetle to opens its wing covers, allowing the pseudoscorpions to climb on. The pseudoscorpions produce a silk-like thread, which they attach to the beetle's back to keep them secure during the flight. Then the beetle takes off, carrying them to their new home.

A harlequin beetle and a tiny pseudoscorpion.

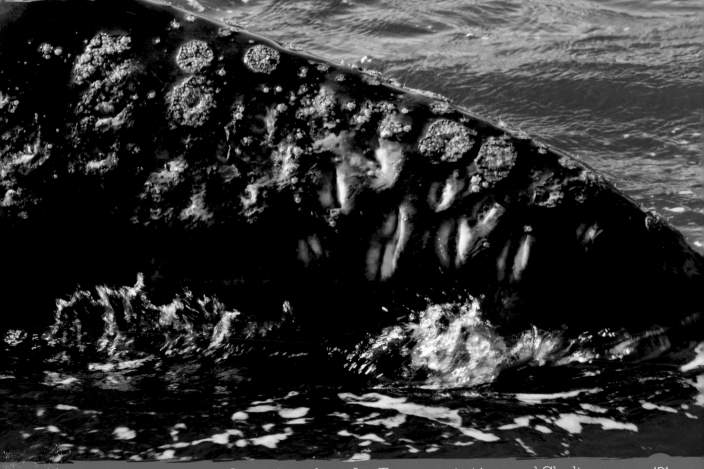

GOPHER TORTOISE

Some creatures make use of homes created and then left behind by animals of another **species.** This is an example of **commensalism,** because the home's creator is not harmed.

The gopher tortoise of the southeastern United States lives in long burrows that it digs with its broad front legs. These burrows help more than 350 species of living things, including other **reptiles,** mice, frogs, **insects,** and **arachnids.** Most are **commensals,** living right inside the tortoise's burrow or digging their own burrows from its sides. Some animals cannot live anywhere else but inside the gopher tortoise's burrows.

HERMIT CRABS

Many species of hermit crab make their homes in the empty shells of ocean-dwelling snails, which they carry with them. The shell protects the crab's soft **abdomen** from **predators.** The crabs' abdomens are curved to fit the spiral shape of the shell, with a small pair of legs at the tip to hook onto the column in the center of the shell. Some hermit crabs will make their homes in the empty shells of other animals, such as clams and scallops.

As a hermit crab grows, it must find larger shells to move into. If there are not enough empty shells to go around, the crabs will fight over them. Crabs that need new shells will sometimes form "vacancy chains." Groups of up to 20 crabs will gather around a large shell and then line up in order of size. They then wait until a crab big enough to claim the shell arrives. That crab moves into the shell, leaving its old shell empty for the next crab in the chain. The move continues down the line, with each crab taking over the shell of the crab in front of it.

Gila woodpecker

The Gila (*HEE lah*) woodpecker is a bird of the desert areas of the southwestern United States and western Mexico. It pecks holes in a type of cactus called saguaro, making a place to lay its **eggs.** When the chicks are grown, they and the parents move out of the nest. A variety of animals may move into the space, including reptiles, **rodents,** and such small birds as elf owls, flycatchers, purple martins, kestrels, and wrens.

Gila woodpeckers carve out a new nest every year, leaving plenty of empty homes for other animals to occupy.

A gopher tortoise outside its burrow. Burrows can be over 40 feet (12 meters) long.

Commensalism for Food

Many small animals find food by living close to larger **hosts.** They may make use of the bigger animal's strength or the way it disturbs the environment as it moves around. They may even get **nutrients** from discarded parts of the animal, such as fur, feathers, or skin.

HELP FROM THE STRONG

Food is hard to come by during the winter months in the Arctic. The caribou (*KAR uh boo*), a large deer, must dig through the snow and earth to eat groups of living things called lichens (*LY kuhnz*), a valuable source of nutrients. The Arctic fox follows the caribou. It takes advantage of the holes the larger animal has dug through the hard ground near the surface. When the caribou has moved on, the fox digs deeper, searching for the burrows of voles, lemmings, and other **rodents.**

The titan triggerfish is a large **species** of fish that lives in lagoons and reefs in the tropical parts of the Indian and Pacific oceans. It often turns over rocks and disturbs sand in its search for food. Smaller fish follow the titan triggerfish, eating the tiny living things it uncovers or stirs up.

A titan triggerfish feeds at a coral reef. Smaller fish follow, hoping for a meal.

Cattle egrets

The cattle egret (*EE greht*) is a species of bird that comes from Africa, but that now lives on every continent except Antarctica. These birds follow large grazing animals, often riding on them. As the grazers brush through long grass or pull it up to eat, they stir up grasshoppers, crickets, spiders, flies, and earthworms for the egrets to eat. This saves the birds the energy needed to search for these creatures in the tall grass.

A cattle egret searches for food at the feet of a grazing cow.

ANTBIRDS

Antbirds are a type of bird found in the forests of Central and South America. They get their name from following lines of army ants. Army ants spend much of their lives on the move, forming into huge **swarms** in their search for **prey. Insects, arachnids,** and other small creatures run or fly away from the swarms, and the antbirds are ready to swoop down and catch them.

For many types of antbird, creatures flushed out by army ants provide just a small part of their diet. But 18 **species** have become entirely dependent on this form of hunting. These specialized antbirds spend their lives following the swarms, and they visit the ants' bivouacs (*BIHV u aks,* temporary nests) each morning to check on their activity. As a result, they tend to be there first when a swarm goes on the move. It is their calls that attract other antbird species to the swarm.

A spotted antbird eating a spider stirred up by a swarm of army ants.

There is a pecking order among followers of the ant swarm. **Dominant** species, such as the ocellated antbird of Central America, position themselves close to the center and front of the swarm, where they can catch the largest amount of prey. Less dominant species will take spots farther from the center or higher up.

Impala and baboon

Sometimes, a **commensal** follows its host not for its size or strength, but for its special abilities. On the African **savanna,** impalas, a type of antelope, are often seen following baboons. When the baboons climb sausage trees (so named because their fruit look like sausages), the impalas will gather below. The baboons peel and eat the fruit, discarding the peel. The waiting impalas eat bits of fruit left over in the peel. The impalas cannot reach the fruit themselves, and even if the fruit falls on its own, they cannot chew through its tough peel.

As well as providing bits of peeled fruit to impalas, baboons also make them safer. The impalas recognize baboon alarm calls, so they know when a predator is approaching.

As a swarm of army ants moves through the leaf litter of the forest, it stirs up many tiny creatures.

DUNG BEETLE

When an animal eats, some parts of its food will pass through its body undigested and end up in its feces. These parts provide **nutritients** for certain kinds of **insects,** including dung beetles.

Some dung beetle **species** eat the feces of many kinds of animals. Others eat the dung of only one kind of animal. They search for dung using their powerful sense of smell. Most dung beetle species are attracted to the feces of plant-eating animals, which contain lots of undigested plant fiber. Dung beetle **larvae** eat the solid parts of the dung, while the adult beetles use their mouthparts to suck the juice from the feces.

Some species of dung beetle form a piece of dung into a ball, which they roll away from the dung pile. They bury the ball for use as a food store or as a place for the female to lay her **eggs.** Other species of dung beetle will bury the dung where they find it. A third type will simply live in the dung.

BURROWING OWL

The burrowing owl has a different kind of **commensalistic** relationship with the dung of large plant eating animals. It does not eat their feces, as the dung beetle does, but instead uses them as bait. The owl places the feces outside its burrow to attract dung beetles. When they arrive to collect the feces, the burrowing owl eats the beetles.

Unlike many owl species, burrowing owls are active in the daytime. They spend much of this time sitting at the entrances to their burrows "fishing" for dung beetles.

A dung beetle rolls its ball by standing on its front legs and pushing the ball with its back legs. It rolls the ball in a perfectly straight line, in some cases using the stars in the sky to guide its path.

SCAVENGERS

A common form of **commensalism** is scavenging—eating the meat of dead animals. The dead animal is the **host** in this relationship, and the **scavenger** is the **commensal.** Some animals rely entirely on scavenging, such as some vultures, burying beetles, and blowflies. Many **predators** also sometimes turn to scavenging. These include hyenas, jackals, lions, leopards, wolves, wild dogs, and crows. Scavengers play an important role in the environment, especially in hot areas. They eat **carcasses** that might otherwise rot and spread disease.

Burying beetles bury the carcasses of small animals, such as birds and **rodents,** to feed their **larvae.** A burying beetle's **antennae** have smelling **organs** that can sense dead animals from far away. After finding a carcass, a burying beetle will often have to fight other burying beetles for it. The males fight males, and the females fight females, until just one male and female are left. The winning pair then buries the carcass before other scavengers can find and steal it.

The beetles bury the carcass by digging a hole around and beneath it. After the burial, they cover the carcass with fluids from their bodies that kill **bacteria** and **fungi.** This slows the decay of the carcass, helping to prevent it from attracting other scavengers. The beetles strip away any fur and feathers, which they use to line the burial chamber (room), and work the carcass into a compact ball. The whole process takes around eight hours.

The female lays her **eggs** in the soil next to the carcass. When the larvae hatch, they enter the carcass through a cone-shaped hole created by the parents, and they begin to eat it. As the larvae grow, the parents continue to tend the carcass, removing fungi and treating the carcass with fluids to slow its decay.

Vultures

Vultures are birds that are well adapted to the life of a scavenger. Their stomachs contain a powerful acid that kills any bacteria in the meat they eat. This adaptation allows them to eat rotting carcasses without getting sick. Some vulture species urinate on their legs. Acid in the urine kills any bacteria that the vulture picks up stepping among carcasses.

A pair of griffon vultures scavenge on a carcass.

A burying beetle on a dead bird.

External Parasites

Animals that gain such benefits as nutrition from another animal at the other animal's expense are known as **parasites.** Some parasites, called **ectoparasites,** live on the outside of or near their **hosts.** Other parasites, called **endoparasites,** live inside their hosts. This section is about ectoparasites.

THE CATERPILLAR AND THE ANTS

Some parasites trick their host into providing them with benefits. Caterpillars of the *Phengaris (fehn GAHR ihs)* butterfly, for example, use **mimicry** to sneak into the nests of certain red ants.

Phengaris caterpillars begin their lives eating the seeds and flowers of such plants as thyme. After a time, they drop to the ground, ready to begin their career as parasites. The caterpillars give off **pheromones** that **mimic** the pheromones of ant **larvae.** Eventually, an ant picks up the caterpillar, thinking it to be a lost larva. The tricked ant carries the caterpillar back to the ants' nest.

Once in the nest, the *Phengaris* caterpillar will make sounds like those of the ant larvae, tricking ant workers into feeding it. One *Phengaris* **species** mimics the sounds of the queen ant. This tricks the worker ants into thinking that the caterpillar is a queen ant larva, and they will feed it and even favor it over the real ant larvae. Some times, worker ants will kill their own larvae to feed to the caterpillar, and they will rescue the caterpillar first if the nest is in danger. Another *Phengaris* species does not wait to be fed by the worker ants. It simply starts eating the ant larvae once it is inside the nest.

Tetramorium inquilinum ant

The **parasitic** ant *Tetramorium inquilinum* (*teh truh MOHR ee uhm ihn kwih LIH nuhm*) fools its host, the pavement ant, into accepting it as part of the pavement ants' **colony.** It does this by sending out chemical signals that mimic the hosts' pheromones. *T. inquilinum* spends most of its adult life clinging to the back of its host. It does not need to find food, as it lives on the liquid food given out by its hosts. It has no worker ants, but only queens and males.

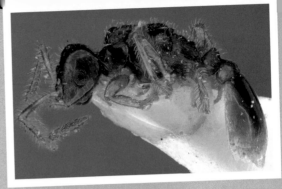

T. inquilinum is a small, frail creature with a shrunken body and large pads and claws for holding onto its host.

An ant looks after a *Phengaris* caterpillar.

PARASITES THAT STEAL

Kleptoparasites are **parasites** that steal food or other things gathered by their **hosts** for themselves or for their young. Many animals will do this once in a while. Bears and gray wolves, for example, might steal the kills of smaller **predators,** like foxes and coyotes, by scaring them away. Bald eagles will steal from other birds of prey, such as ospreys.

Skuas often steal the catches of other seabirds, such as gulls and terns. Once another bird has caught a fish, the fast, acrobatic skua chases it until it drops its catch. Sometimes, skuas fly as a group, targeting a single bird. Frigatebirds hover high above **colonies** of nesting seabirds. When a parent bird arrives with food for its young, the frigatebird dives in to attack the bird and steal its food.

A magnificent frigatebird stealing food from a red-billed tropicbird.

Diving birds are often targeted as soon as they surface with food. Seabirds called Heermann's gulls will grab small fish escaping from a brown pelican's bill as it surfaces. Similarly, American coots will steal from the bills of diving ducks.

The tiny spider *Mysmenopsis furtiva* (*mihs mehn OHP sihs fur TEE vuh*) lives in the web of another spider, *Ischnothele xera* (*isk noh THEHL ay ZEHR uh*), stealing some of its host's **prey.** Spiders are usually able to sense any outsider through vibrations in their webs. The kleptoparasite avoids being discovered by not moving or by moving very slowly when the host is motionless. When the host moves, *M. furtiva* is able to make more rapid movements, because the host spider cannot tell the kleptoparasite's vibrations apart from its own. *M. furtiva* waits for the host to capture its prey, then joins it at the feeding site. Sometimes, the host stops eating to attack or chase away the smaller spider, but it may be unable to rid itself of the thief in its web.

Slave-making ants

Slave-making ants kidnap ants from other colonies and force them to work for them. To get slaves, the slave-makers carry out raids on other colonies. The raiding party includes both slave-makers and slaves kidnapped from other host colonies. Raids are usually successful because the slave-making ants give off **pheromones** that cause the **colony** defenders to attack one another. But the slave-makers don't always get their way. Sometimes, enslaved host workers will fight back by killing slave-maker **pupae.**

Slave-making ants and their orange ant slaves in an acorn.

On the African savanna, spotted hyenas and lions often steal each other's kills.

The Cuckoo: Brood Parasite

A brood parasite is an animal that tricks another animal into raising its young. The brood parasite then can spend more of its energy on other activities, such as looking for food and **mates.** Some birds, **insects,** and fish are brood parasites. One of the most well-known brood parasites is a bird called the cuckoo.

The female cuckoo watches a possible **host** from a nearby perch, waiting for it to lay its **eggs.** Host birds include magpies, warblers, dunnocks, bramblings, and robins. When the host leaves the nest, the cuckoo flies in and lays an egg. Sometimes it removes one of the host's eggs at the same time. The cuckoo then plays no further part in its chick's rearing.

The cuckoo chick often hatches earlier than the host's chicks. Soon after hatching, it usually pushes the host's eggs or hatchlings out of the nest. That way, it gets all of the host bird's attention. Cuckoo chicks make loud begging calls when opening their beaks for food, and many have brightly colored mouths, which probably encourages the host to bring more food. The cuckoo chick grows quickly, often becoming bigger than its host parent.

A REED WARBLER host feeds a young cuckoo.

Host bird **species** have developed defenses against the cuckoo's trickery. If a cuckoo is sighted near a nest, host birds may let out alarm calls and drive it away. Some host bird species, such as the brambling, have **evolved** the ability to recognize cuckoo eggs, and they will remove them from the nest. Cuckoos who target bramblings have adapted to this defense by producing eggs that look more like brambling eggs.

In Australia, a species of bird called the superb fairy wren has evolved a clever way of defending itself against the cuckoo. The mother teaches a certain call to its chicks while they are still in the egg. This song works like a password. The mother wren knows that once they hatch, the chicks that can make this call must be her own young.

BLOODSUCKERS

Many **parasites** live on or attach themselves to the skin of bigger animals and suck their blood. Examples include fleas, lice, mosquitoes, mites, ticks, leeches, and vampire bats. Some of these animals can make their **hosts** sick.

Ticks are small **arachnids.** They find their hosts by following the odor of the animal's breath or sweat. They lie in wait in a position known as questing. They cling to leaves and grass with their rear legs while holding their forelimbs outstretched, waiting to grasp the host and climb onto it. Some ticks attach to the host right away. Others wander around searching for thinner skin, such as on the host's ears. Ticks may stay attached for days or weeks, drinking the host's blood and swelling up in size.

In many mosquito **species,** the female must have a meal of blood before she can lay **eggs.** Mosquitoes find their hosts by using their senses of sight and smell, and by picking up the heat of the animal. The mosquito's mouthparts make up a tubelike structure called a proboscis (*proh BOS ihs).* Six needlelike mouthparts, called stylets, are covered and protected by the **insect's** lower lip, called the labium (*LAY bee uhm).* As the stylets enter the skin, the labium bends and slides upward out of the way.

The mosquito then releases saliva into the wound through channels formed by the stylets. Blood usually clots—or forms a thick, sticky mass—if it is exposed to substances from outside the body. But the mosquito's saliva contains substances that keep the blood from clotting, allowing the mosquito to suck more blood from the wound. After the mosquito has drunk enough blood, it slowly pulls the stylets from the wound, and the labium slips into place over them.

Vampire bat

The common vampire bat feeds mainly on the blood of **mammals.** Once it finds its host, it searches for a warm spot on the skin to bite. It uses its canine and cheek teeth to shave away any hair or fur. Then it uses a pair of razor-sharp upper front teeth to cut through the skin, lapping up the blood that flows from the wound. As with the mosquito, the bat's saliva contains a chemical to prevent the blood from clotting. A bat can consume half its body weight in blood during a 20-minute feeding.

A vampire bat baring its extremely sharp upper teeth.

A female tick in questing position.

Internal Parasites

Parasites that live inside their **hosts** are called **endoparasites.** They may make their homes in the host's body **tissues,** blood vessels, or digestive system. Some endoparasites spend their lives inside a single host. Others must move between different hosts to complete their life cycle. Some endoparasites will even influence their host's behavior to help in their move to another host.

PARASITIC WORMS

Parasitic worms are creatures that live in the intestines and sometimes the blood vessels of their hosts. They include roundworms, thorny-headed worms, and flatworms. These creatures live by absorbing **nutrients** from their hosts, often leaving the host weakened and likely to get sick. Parasitic worms can live for years inside their hosts, giving off chemicals that prevent the host's immune system from attacking them. The parasites' **eggs** are passed with the host's feces and may then spread to new hosts.

Some roundworms live on their own in the environment. Others are parasites and must live inside a plant or animal host. Roundworms have thin, tubelike bodies that range in size from microscopic to over 3 feet (90 centimeters) long. They can enter a host as eggs, **larvae,** or as adults. Some enter the host in its food. Other **species** enter through the bite of an **insect.** In certain roundworm species, the larva enters a host by burrowing through its skin.

The tapeworm is a type of flatworm that lives in the digestive systems of **vertebrates.** Its eggs enter a host in food or drink. The eggs hatch, and the worms attach themselves to the host's intestinal wall with suckers or hooks. They absorb nutrients from the host's food through their skin. Eggs leave the host in its feces.

Blood-fluke

Blood-flukes are flatworms that live in the blood vessels. They hatch in water contaminated with feces and enter a tiny snail host. After growing inside the snail for a time, the larvae come back out into the water and burrow through the skin of a larger host. Once inside the larger host, the blood-flukes grow into their adult form, feed on blood, and find another blood-fluke to **mate** with. The female then lays thousands of eggs. Any eggs that are not expelled in the host's feces get lodged in its internal **organs** and can cause swelling and tissue damage.

A blood-fluke.

Fully grown tapeworms have a flat, ribbonlike appearance.

COMPLEX LIFE CYCLES

Blood-flukes are not the only **endoparasites** to depend on more than one **species** to complete their life cycles. Many **parasites** go through different stages in their growth inside different hosts. For example, a parasite's **eggs** may hatch into **larvae** inside one host species, and the larvae may grow into adult parasites inside another.

The green-banded broodsac is a **parasitic** flatworm whose life cycle uses both a bird and a snail. The adult flatworm lives and reproduces in a bird's digestive system. Its eggs are released in the bird's droppings, which are then eaten by snails.

Inside the snail, the egg hatches into a long white structure called a sporocyst (*SPAWR uh sihst*). The sporocyst attaches itself to the snail's digestive system and grows by absorbing **nutrients** from the snail through its skin. To complete its life cycle, the parasite must then make sure that the snail is eaten by a bird. So the sporocyst sends out long tubes called broodsacs, filled with larvae, which tunnel into one of the snail's tentacles. The tentacle swells up and turns bright colors. To a bird, this may look like a juicy caterpillar.

To improve its chances of being eaten, the parasite gives off chemicals that are picked up by the snail's brain, changing its behavior. The snail, normally active at night, becomes active in the daytime. It moves onto the upper parts of plants and other exposed places where it is likely to be spotted by a bird. When a bird sees the tentacle, it swoops down and bites it off. The worms grow into adults inside the bird, and the cycle begins again.

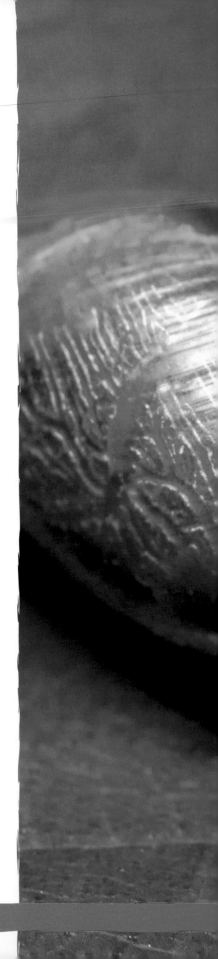

Slime balls

The lancet liver fluke needs three hosts to complete its life cycle. The adult fluke lives in the intestines of cattle and sheep. Its eggs leave the host in feces, which are eaten by a snail. The eggs hatch into larvae inside the snail. The body of the snail tries to defend itself against the invaders by wrapping the larvae in capsules called cysts *(sihsts)*. The snail releases the cysts in balls of slime from its skin. The slime balls are eaten by ants, who are attracted to the slime trails of snails for their moisture. The larvae have a way to make their ant hosts move to the tops of blades of grass and stay there, where they are likely to be eaten by grazing cows or sheep.

Adult lancet liver fluke seen under a microscope.

A snail infected by the green-banded broodsac.

THE HORSEHAIR WORM AND THE CRICKET

Another **parasite** that changes the behavior of its **host** is a **species** of horsehair worm. The worm begins its life as an **egg** in a lake or river. After two weeks, a **larva** hatches from the egg. It cannot swim, so the larva waits to be eaten by the larva of a flying **insect,** such as a mayfly or mosquito. The host larva grows into an adult flying insect, while the horsehair worm larva waits inside of it. Only if the host insect is eaten by a cricket will the larva be able to complete its life cycle.

If the horsehair worm larva gets inside a cricket, it digs into the cricket's body and takes in **nutrients** from the cricket's digestive system. In the process, the tiny larva grows into an adult worm up to 1 foot (30 centimeters) in length.

The infected cricket's appearance stays the same, but the worm begins to change its host's behavior. The cricket stops chirping, something that uses up energy that could otherwise be used to feed the parasite. Chirping would also make the cricket more noticeable to its **predators,** threatening the parasite inside it.

The worm also changes the cricket's attitude towards water. Instead of avoiding bodies of water, the cricket starts looking for them. Once it finds a lake or river, the cricket throws itself in. Then the long, spaghetti-like horsehair worm bores a hole through the cricket's body and squirms out. The worm swims around until it finds a **mate.** After mating, the female lays her eggs underwater, and the cycle begins again. Remarkably, if the cricket can avoid drowning, it can survive and recover!

Ladybug bodyguards

A type of **parasitic** wasp gets ladybugs to guard its **pupae** from predators. The wasp stings the ladybug and deposits an egg inside it. When the egg hatches, the larva eats its way out through the body of the still-living ladybug, coming out through the **abdomen.** The larva then spins itself a **cocoon** between the ladybug's legs. It stays there for six to nine days before coming out as an adult wasp. During this period, the ladybug's brightly colored body scares off predators. If a predator approaches, the ladybug will thrash and twitch its limbs. Scientists are not sure why the host does this, but many think it is due to some kind of control by the parasite.

A ladybug protecting the cocoon of a wasp. Remarkably, a quarter of ladybugs survive such an infection.

A horsehair worm comes out of an infected cricket.

THE BARNACLE AND THE CRAB

Most barnacles attach to hard surfaces—sometimes large animals (see page 16)—and filter out food from ocean water. But one type, *Sacculina* (*sak yew LEE nuh*), has developed a strange **parasitic** relationship with some types of crabs. A female *Sacculina* **larva** finds a crab and crawls along it until it finds a joint in the crab's shell. The larva then sheds its hard shell and injects its soft, sluglike body into the crab.

Once inside, *Sacculina* spreads tendrils (thin, threadlike growths) through the crab's **abdomen** to suck **nutrients.** To take as many of the crab's nutrients for itself as possible, *Sacculina* sends out other tendrils to surround its **host's** nervous system. These tendrils give off substances that make the crab unable to molt (shed its shell before growing a new one), grow, reproduce, or regrow lost limbs. The crab is now completely controlled by the **parasite.**

If *Sacculina* has taken over a male crab, it will give off chemicals that change the crab's appearance and behavior to that of a female crab. For example, it will widen and flatten the crab's abdomen and even make the crab perform female **mating** dances. *Sacculina* turns the crab into a female so that its abdomen forms a better shape for hosting the **parasite's eggs** and so it takes better care of the eggs. After a few weeks, *Sacculina* grows a pouch containing its eggs that hangs out of the rear of the crab's abdomen. Free-swimming male *Sacculina* find this pouch and **fertilize** the eggs.

The crab, under the complete control of *Sacculina*, will care for the parasite's eggs. When they are ready to hatch, the crab climbs onto a high rock, as it would do as part of its own reproductive cycle. But instead of releasing its own eggs into the sea, it releases the *Sacculina* eggs. An infected crab may even raise multiple batches of *Sacculina* eggs in its lifetime.

A crab taken over by *Sacculina* carries the parasitic barnacle's egg pouch beneath its abdomen.

Tongue-eating louse

The tongue-eating louse is the only parasite we know about that takes over an entire **organ** inside its host. It enters the host fish through its gills, where it lives until it reaches adulthood. Then it climbs inside the fish's mouth and attaches itself to the tongue. It bites the tongue and sucks blood out of it, causing the tongue to shrivel away. The louse then replaces the tongue, feeding off the fish's blood and mouth **mucus.** The fish, meanwhile, continues to live and eat as normal.

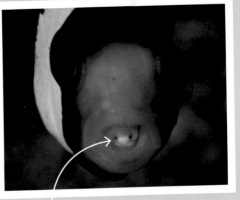

A tongue-eating louse has replaced the tongue of this saddleback anemonefish.

PARASITES THAT KILL

Some **parasites,** known as parasitoids, end up killing their **hosts.** The lancet liver fluke (see page 39) is one example, changing the behavior of its ant host so that it gets eaten. This most extreme form of dependence on another animal is similar to predation (hunting).

A well-known example of a parasitoid is the emerald cockroach wasp, which turns a living cockroach into a meal for its offspring. The female wasp hunts down a cockroach and bites it while aiming a sting between the first pair of the cockroach's legs. This sting **paralyzes** the cockroach for a while, giving the wasp time to aim a second sting directly into the cockroach's brain. The second sting can take up to a minute as the wasp steers its stinger around inside the cockroach's head, seeking the precise point where its **venom** must go.

The venom changes the cockroach's behavior, leaving it calm and easily handled. First, the cockroach cleans itself. Some scientists think this cleaning behavior makes sure that the wasp **larva** gets a germ-free meal. While the cockroach is busy cleaning itself, the wasp goes in search of a small hole in the ground where it can bury the cockroach. The wasp returns and breaks off the cockroach's **antennae,** drinking some of its body fluid for energy. Then it bites down on the stub of an antenna and leads the powerless cockroach to the hole in the ground.

Once the cockroach has been pushed into the hole, the wasp lays an **egg** on its leg before sealing it up inside. After two days, the egg hatches and the wasp larva chews its way inside the cockroach. It eats the cockroach's internal **organs** one by one until the cockroach finally dies.

Hyperparasitoids

Parasitoids sometimes become hosts to other parasitoids, known as hyperparasitoids. One example of a hyperparasitoid is a wasp that lays its eggs in the **pupae** of another type of parasitoid wasp, which itself lays its eggs inside a caterpillar. The hyperparasitoid wasp tracks down its host by smell. Plants attacked by caterpillars infected by the parasitoid wasp give off a slightly different scent than do those attacked by uninfected caterpillars. By sensing this difference, the hyperparasitoid wasp can find the caterpillars that contain the host it needs.

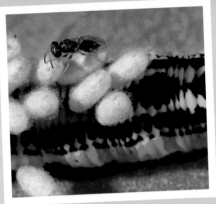

A hyperparasitoid wasp on the cocoons of parasitoid wasps attached to a caterpillar.

An emerald cockroach wasp leads a cockroach away to be eaten by the wasp's young.

Glossary

abdomen the rear part of an arthropod's body.

alga (plural algae) a simple living thing that can make its own food.

antenna (plural antennae) a long, delicate sense organ, or feeler, found on the heads of various invertebrates, including insects.

arthropod a very large group of invertebrates with jointed legs that includes insects, arachnids, and crustaceans.

arachnid a family of arthropods that includes spiders and scorpions.

bacterium (plural bacteria) a single-celled living thing. Some bacteria can cause disease.

carcass the dead body of an animal.

client an animal that benefits from the services of a cleaning animal.

cocoon a covering made of soft threads spun by some insects as protection during the pupa stage, as they change into adults.

colony a group of living things of one species that live together or grow in the same place.

commensal a living thing that exhibits commensalism.

commensalism a symbiotic relationship in which one species benefits and the other is not affected.

dominant having power or influence over another.

ectoparasite a parasite that lives on the outside of or near its host.

egg a female sex cell, or the structure in which the embryo develops, usually outside the mother's body.

endoparasite a parasite that lives inside of its host.

evolve in a living thing, to change or develop over the course of many generations.

fertilize to join sperm from a male with egg from a female so that a young animal develops.

fungus (plural fungi) a living thing that usually grows on plants or on decaying matter. Yeast and mushrooms are fungi.

host a living thing that is either harmed or not affected in a symbiotic relationship.

insect one of the major invertebrate groups. Invertebrate animals do not have a backbone. Insects have six legs and a three-part body.

larva (plural larvae) the active, immature stage of some animals, such as many insects, that is different from its adult form.

mammal one of the major vertebrate animal groups. Mammals feed their offspring on milk produced by the mother, and most have hair or fur.

mate the animal with which another animal partners to reproduce (to make more animals like the two that are mating); the act of mating, when two animals come together to reproduce.

mimic to copy something, or the close external resemblance of an animal to something else; an animal that does this.

mimicry the action of copying something, or the close external resemblance of an animal to something else.

mucus a thick liquid that is produced in parts of animals' bodies.

mutualistic, mutualism a symbiotic relationship in which both species benefit.

nutrient a substance that is needed to keep a living thing alive and help it grow.

organ a part of the body, made of similar cells and cell tissue, that performs a particular function.

paralyze to make a living thing unable to move.

parasite a living thing that lives on or inside another living thing, such as an animal or plant, and gets its food from it.

parasitic, parasitism a symbiotic relationship in which one species benefits and the other is harmed.

pheromone a chemical substance linked to the sense of smell given out by an animal as a signal to others in its species.

predator an animal that hunts, kills, and eats other animals.

prey an animal that is hunted, killed, and eaten by another.

pupa (plural pupae) an insect in the stage of development between a larva and an adult insect.

reptile one of the major vertebrate animal groups. A reptile has dry, scaly skin and breathes air. Snakes, crocodiles, and lizards are all reptiles.

rodent a mammal with front teeth made for gnawing hard things.

savanna grasslands with widely scattered bushes and trees.

scavenger an animal that feeds on the carcasses of dead animals.

species a group of living things that have certain permanent traits in common and are able to reproduce with each other.

sub-Saharan Africa the part of Africa south of the Sahara Desert.

swarm a large group of arthropods moving together either in search of food or a new home.

symbiosis, symbiotic relationship a relationship between two species from which at least one benefits.

tissue the material of which living things are made.

venom a naturally produced liquid that animals can introduce into other animals (for example, through biting) in order to stun, injure, or kill the other animal.

vertebrate an animal with a backbone.

BOOKS

Body Snatchers: Flies, Wasps, and Other Creepy Crawly Zombie Makers (Real-Life Zombies) by Joan Axelrod-Contrada (Capstone Press, 2016)

Symbiosis: How Different Animals Relate (Big Science Ideas) by Bobbie Kalman (Crabtree, 2016)

Top 10: Partnerships (Wild Wicked Wonderful) by Virginia Loh-Hagan (45th Parallel Press, 2017)

Zombie Caterpillars (Zombie Animals: Parasites Take Control!) by Frances Nagle (Gareth Stevens, 2015)

WEBSITES

BBC Science – Parasitism and Mutualism
http://www.bbc.co.uk/schools/gcsebitesize
/science/edexcel/problems_in_environment
/interdependencerev4.shtml
A brief introduction to different kinds of animal interdependence.

National Geographic – Ant and Butterfly Symbiosis
http://video.nationalgeographic.com/video/ant
_caterpillarsymbiosis
Watch this video featuring spectacular close-ups of an ant-caterpillar symbiosis in action.

Queensland Museum – Competition and Commensalism
http://www.qm.qld.gov.au/Find+out+about
/Animals+of+Queensland/Sea+Life/
Learn about the symbiosis between a variety of ocean animals.